Seasons of Thought

Seasons of Thought

D.S. Chapman

Copyright ©2019 Daniel Chapman. All Rights Reserved.

Published by Daniel Chapman – 1st edition

Cover Design by Zachary Tullsen

Except for brief quotations, no part of this book may be reproduced in any manner without prior written permission from the publisher. Email: permissions@dschapman.com

ISBN 978-0-578-50435-3

www.dschapman.com

They looked at all the summer shelved and glimmering there in the motionless streams, the bottles of dandelion wine. Numbered from one to ninety-odd there the ketchup bottles, most of them full now, stood burning in the cellar twilight one for every living summer day.

"Boy," said Tom, "what a swell way to save June, July, and August. Real practical."
Dandelion Wine, Ray Bradbury

Glory be to God for dappled things –
For skies of couple-colour as a brinded cow;
For rose-moles all in stipple upon trout that swim;
Fresh-firecoal chestnut-falls; finches' wings;
Landscape plotted and pieced – fold, fallow, and plough;
And áll trádes, their gear and tackle and trim.
Pied Beauty, Gerard Manley Hopkins

Contents

On Poetry...1
Winter..3
    The Hearth......................................4
    Advent..5
    Comatose..6
    The Fox...7
    Jazz Quartet on Christmas Eve..............8
    Static...9
    The Grand Tour................................10
    Breath..11
Interlude...13
    On the Human Soul...........................14
Spring..15
    Bird Song...16
    Meaning..17
    The Man with the Plunger.................18
    Petrichor...19
    The Top..20
    Soap..21
    The Gardener..................................22
    Evening Praise.................................23
Interlude...25
    On the Human Mind........................26
Summer..29
    The Engineer...................................30
    Berry Picking..................................31
    Another..32
    Halcyon..33
    Calligraphy.....................................34
    Baptism..35
    Riverbend.......................................36
Interlude...37
    On the Human Body........................38
Autumn..39
    Sunset...40
    Evergreen..41

Stars	42
Traffic	43
Touseled	44
Narration	45
Apple Dumplings	46
Time	47
Winter's Reprise	**49**
Snowfall	50

On Poetry

"What do you see?"
>The branch of an almond tree,
>A boiling pot tilted to the north.

First the images, later the meaning–
>coals placed on tongues,
>descending doves,

a kingdom inside a mustard seed
>turrets pressed close against the shell,
>ready to sprout into towers,

bread like flesh.

What do I see?
>I see the Poet
>speaking as if to poets.

Winter

The Hearth

Can words still kiss, or has the spark fled?
Do their voices crack, bounce like empty shells?
Or after all this time can they sit still
in the same room
speaking love
in silence?

Advent

There is a cold we cannot shake–
caught in the air, imprisoned
in the wood of the bedroom floor–
It spreads its iron chains
till it freezes our lungs.
Our feet lose all their feeling.

There is a cold we cannot shake
even after we come inside
shedding frozen air like a coat.
It abides in our chests,
freezes our lips when we cough.

We are the frozen people,
caught with a cold that lingers
even in the heat of summer.
Our toes and tongue ache for warm
freedom, long evaporated.

There is still warmth–
lingering in a loaf of bread,
woven between the glass of wine
and conversation over dinner.
The ice remains to our core,

warmed for a passing moment,
but aching for a great thaw,
for the warmth of blankets and stoves,
the thawing of lips and feet–
longing for the coming of a flame.

Comatose

The grass sways with the sickly yellow face
of an invalid longing for the sun,
laid up in the fever room, wrapped and tied
with ice, lest the patient's heart start to run.
The healthy green of summer has been drained.
Now the heavens don the mournful drapes
of the deep sleep which can not be feigned.
Surely winter kills life with steady scrapes
of white claws? Must we wait for the spring thaw
for life to again bubble from the earth?
Or perhaps the grass sways with suppressed mirth
from the sudden sound of the crow's guffaw.
Winter covers all with a cold embrace,
but death purges all without any trace.

The Fox

lights freeze the red fox
in the grayscale of twilight
sound fades to silence

Jazz Quartet on Christmas Eve

The rain snapped a snare drum beat on the thatch.
Its steady tip tap echoed from the top

till it hit the ears of the two stabled
together beneath the straw with a splash.

One drop made no difference on her brow, drenched
with the drained sweat from her young pain-drawn face.

The beat of the jazz quartet continued;
two slow trumpets from a neighboring stall

joined the stable snare, improvising round
the last member of this impromptu band,

whose high wailing voice in a minor key
and impassioned face painted the pain

of the world as her husband looked on, wishing
to conduct the band in this song he could

not play, but supporting his singing wife
with shaking hands and eyes steady in love.

There was no silence in the barn that night
only a song that ripped at more than ears,

backed by the melancholy beat of years
accustomed to such violent agony.

Static

The air is charged.
        Step out and feel
the electric energy of the cold.

Breathe in the dry caffeine of winter,
        cleansed of all moisture,
smelling only of air.

The leaves feel it too
        as they bounce on the cold concrete
              powered by the cool current of the North.

The Grand Tour

"Have you ever thought about what comes next?"
        Grandpa said three months before he found out.
"I think an angel will take me about
        the earth before beginning the great trek
to the stars," he said, putting National
        Geographic down and sitting up, or
as far up as his bent back allowed before
        stopping short, his eyes were affable
as he always was, "He'll fly me past Mars,
        we'll skim the deep clouds of Saturn,
then he'll race out with me wrapped in his arms
        as the stars fade in a quilted pattern."
He finished. I don't know what to say.
        I hope that I'll see what he saw one day.

Breath

There has been a wind blowing off the Atlantic,
whipping through the sidewalks of the east,
driving all with relentless force towards home.
It bursts into the bars on Friday night
hitting the back corner where four sit in a warm knot.
The wind joins the conversation,
knitting and purling with the human heart
a chord of friendship laced with laughter.

There's a breeze coming off the Pacific
pulling at the white lace of a coastal wedding,
gracing the ceremony with a gentle dance.
It pushes the backs of volunteers
girding their arms to pull victims from the mud.
It even comes to the gridlocked highways
weaving through their stagnant exhaust
to meld its song with the car stereo.

There is a breath out and about
roaming the planet disguised as wind.
It is related to the common human spirit,
but it is something more
which broods over human hearts
whispering in their ears
with the harsh strength of a blizzard's gust,
the fierce mighty power of a hurricane,
and the quiet warm voice of a summer breeze.

If you listen with expectation
it will rattle down the asphalt of the cul-de-sac
even in the still dead air of January.

Interlude

On the Human Soul

When the soul has fled from its earthly home
        to join its maker in that great abode,
what is its state and what's inside the load
        it carries to the infinite shalom
from the world of din? What is the imprint
        of the flesh database inside our skulls,
with all the records kept of who we'd been
        and what we'd seen before our rotting hulls
let in the sea of time? Do we go in
        blank, washed of the scars of mental trauma,
cleansed too of the joyous human drama
        of loss then love which drew us tightly in?
Or is the spirit pressed in mem'ry's ink
with a stamp that changes how we think?

Spring

Bird Song

The evening sky resounds with grace
        the echoing fullness of a closing day,
        which on inspection was the same
        amalgamation of dissonant chords
        and harsh wasting words as always.
Yet the song birds still chant up their praise
        which rises till it resonates
        sending the shivers of their song in colors
        humming at the frequency of joy,
despite anything I try to say to the contrary.

Meaning

Did you ever stop and wonder,
what's entailed in a name?
Why some are filled with curses,
and others filled with fame?

Did you ever pause and ponder
at the greatness in a word,
how the names of those who
do good things are pleasant when they're heard?

Pray, stop and consider,
the power held in a phrase.
Has no one ever used three words,
which left your heart amazed?

What if each lonely letter
said more about a friend
than every crafted résumé
she would ever send?

If names could hold such meaning,
I'd relish every sound.
I'd tap at every consonant
until the soul resounds.

The Man with the Plunger

The slow turning of this world makes us all sick.
We spun quickly in childhood, strands of spaghetti
flung out like arms. We whirled as we ate up life.
Either the spinning or the eating made us sick
and though we stopped, the world taunts us with its spinning,
as if years ago a cat knocked a ball of yarn
down a hill. Most of the yarn is gone but it still
tumbles on. Entropy can't be stopped.
Even now, in its old age, it's faster than us all.

I saw an old man caught off guard by entropy's
ambush. Leather shoes thrown on under plaid sweatpants,
sun hat tied tightly under chin, he strode on
despite the earth which spun to trip him up, and cars
which tumbled by at the behest of gravity.
He marched to war, plunger tipped like a gun at rest.
He went, despite his age, to stem the spinning flood.

Petrichor

The afternoon after the storm smells of dirt
mixed with the scent of processed petrichor
which rises from the shattered lightning
with the stained glass sound of spring.

The Top

Phrases turn to meet their twisting needs
till like a spinning wobbling top
the meaning falls away.

This is the game at which we play
like children in the rain,
who spin and laugh and spin again—
why should they ever change?

The gyre spins the ship around
in part because it can.
To question it, to tame the wind
is beyond the scope of man.

The world it laughs with every wind,
it cries with every gull,
it spins with every lover's heart,
and with their children falls.
The very force that turns the world
is turning at us all.

Soap

A simple solution
   mostly water
      a few basic compounds
      add only breath
           and we all will float like bubbles

The Gardener

The Gardener took me to his field,
"What do you see?" he said, his voice quiet.
But all I could see was the overpass
and figures walking across the glass bridge.
So I said, seeing only road and glass,
"I see a black snake and men in cages."
But the voice repeated, "What do you see?"
"I see land unworked, people far from soil."
My car passed beneath the bridge, but he asked
as I drove down the highway, what I had seen.
So I, knowing that many images
are tired and worn with tire tracks, slept.
In sleep I pondered new ways to answer
and so extract the message from the scene.
How could I fit the sun, bridge, and figures
together in a new, beautiful way?
But when he again asked what I had seen
I said, "an overpass over the road."

Evening Praise

Night skies, bright moon,
stars that pierce the soul
pricking a tear at each puncture–
sweet as well-spent sweat.
    For I forgot how good it is
    to praise the Lord.

Interlude

On the Human Mind

Do you think that God only speaks
to those whose minds are right?
That only those who can discern
meaning from a maze of words
will emerge to behold his face?

No sane man watches God walk in the wind
or learns to worship from the cat's oblation,
yet some can only view the maze from a branch
where they perch making song with the cuckoo.
Their song is simply different from the owl
but both are regarded as the sparrow—
when the wind takes their wings they must sing.

We curse the wind
It blinds our sight
Our mind is pinned
Without the light
We cannot see
In our blind flight
We lose belief

Without the construct of a hedge
to hedge our mental betting spree,
we wander like we saw it still
along the same, loved, well-worn tracks
and even then our God will grow
no larger than our maze was pruned.

There they go round the mulberry bush,
the mulberry bush, the mulberry bush.
There they go round the mulberry bush,
for that is what they can do.

The mind can get in the way,
of feeling the surf and the spray,
but if you see a cat
and can meet him in that
then the hedge is too small to stay.

I am not one to advocate the tearing down of hedges,
but perhaps in the pruning of our manicured lives,
in our constant snipping at the fringe element,
we have cut off buds which might bloom to flowers
more beautiful than we can ever comprehend.

In silencing the cuckoo
we silence one who has met God
and was left with song.

Summer

The Engineer

The child plays unaware in the sunlight
building up a pile of wood and stones
to an ugly assortment,
piled in a junkyard of unwanted scraps.

The yard is the child's kingdom.
The heap of rotting logs
tipped against a tree–her future fort.
Buried in the heart of a shrub
is a growing arboreal palace,
and swaying high in a pine tree–
a watchtower where she can see
three kingdoms over.

Even there he is beside her as a master craftsman,
measuring planks and laying stones,
peering with the engineer over the parapet
to marvel at the rolling earth.
Do not only say,
"Let the little child come to him"
For he was already there,
laughing in a ray of sunshine.

Berry Picking

How do you choose your favorite color?

"If you swing a bucket fast
no berries will drop out."
> *Look for the flash of blue*
> *falling to the earth from the silver ship.*

I did, but I saw only the blue sky,
the twinkle in two blue eyes
and only after I stretched and jumped
peering into the ship
did I see the crew of berries–
blue and calm as a mountain lake,
fresh and sweeter than water.

Another

Without another eye
to move my gaze from where it rests
I would not see the little things;
my words could not astonish me.

Without another ear
to hear the words I thought I said
I would not care to check my thoughts;
I would not think to fear the truth.

Without another voice
to question what I really meant
and push against my words with words,
the tongue would hush within my mind.

But eye, and ear, and voice, and mind
combine to find a fitting form
to bring before their foreign friend –
a poem to surprise us both.

Halcyon

These are the halcyon days of summer–
the time between storms and reaping heat.

Here the cherry clouds form, ripe with spitting pits,
blowing with playful breezes 'bout the bay
of bright inflated plastic.
                        On the lawn the wet
plumes of the liquid peacock splay on the grass
printed in ridiculous grandeur like pages,
the pages bent like backs.
                      The pages bend
to tell rambling tales,
                  aged lips whisper.
In the cool heat they bend, we all bend to a hot fall,

but not yet, as the watermelon plumps,
not here as the summer grows to a clear, wet day.
Now the nesting bird grows tall on her perch,
puffed by her incubating foliage, puffed like a cloud,

and so we all totter,
                  on the brink of equilibrium.

Calligraphy

The brush bristles with ink,
night held in a droplet
too small to see,
balled up like
a black kitten
pouncing
on each
letter.

Baptism

He laughed when he was baptized.
The incongruity of water on his Sunday best,
thoughts of summer water fights at war with Sunday solemnity–
he knows the significance of today.
How could he know and so he laughs;
the water soaks into his chest.

Riverbend

Freedom is a salmon making its way downstream.
The entire river is his to swim,
pausing where the current slows,
floating where the sun cuts through water like stained glass.
He can swim above the rocks at breakneck speeds
or pause for a nap in the cool mud.

Freedom is the walls of the riverbank
that keep the water cold and close.
Freedom is interwoven molecules
that lock out the killing breath above.

Freedom is our journey down the trail
within the locked curving water road,
swimming each in our own way, at our own pace,
riding the current at long last to the sea.

Interlude

On the Human Body

Put away the cameras.
Hide away the pen.
Minimize the digital.
The scene will soon begin.

Life is not a drama,
not in the way you think.
It is the wind that whips your hair
and muffles the words you speak.

Life is in clammy fingers
which slide against the palm,
but you wouldn't have it differently
even if your heart was calm.

We do not need their sensors
to show how life should be;
the eye takes better pictures
with nothing in between.

For life will fit no medium.
No poem rocks a crib.
It cannot quite be painted.
In the end it is only lived.

Autumn

Sunset

Drained, dropping, the screen is fading,
music ending, bar is closing.
Final curtain call is coming.
Light is waning. Light is waning.

Water falling without purpose
sometimes frozen, sometimes soaking,
freezing one day, hot the other.
Drums keep playing. Light is waning.

Words continue through the darkness—
movie kisses, backstage lovers—
silence in the writer's workshop
save a tapping through the shadow.

Light is fading over ocean
as one lover leaves the gangplank.
Ship is casting off at nightfall.
Love is constant. (Is it waning?)

Love is constant, through the waning
though its form is always changing,
shining though the curtain closes
even when it never opens.

Drain a life to dregs of sadness
it will echo to a rhythm.
Feet are tapping, lips are thrumming
even while this light is waning.

Evergreen

The heart of a tree creaks when the breeze comes in too fast.

Perhaps it cries as the breeze reminds it that it will die
        long, tall, and proud as its life might be.

Perhaps it is a battle cry that resounds through sap and wood
        the rage of stability confronted with wild wind.

Maybe, but when I hear the evergreens sigh
as the wind pulls their branches back and forth,
I hear a giant remembering the first time
the wind pulled at his roots.
I hear his heart break and fill
as mine does,
for I, like him,
remember home.

Stars

Blank now, though once lit,
Stars chiseled out from black slate.
The moon sits, carving.

Traffic

Stay in the lines, don't shift without warning.
Stop at the red, right before the thick line.
It's a stop and go game that we play.
Cross a bridge and see what I mean.
The red river stretches stagnant below
the arch of the bridge. Not a drop budges
beyond its banks. Then in a wave the fires
wink out as the columns march
onward in unwavering lines.

March, color, stay in the lines–all is fine.
Are lines insufficient? They can be grown,
stretched in two, even in three dimensions.
Skyscrapers, roads, cubicles–what are they?
Implementations of linear thought.
Take the derivative of efficiency
and you will always get a line.
Come to the bridge and watch this calculus at work

or look up and see the lost red-tailed hawk waste its life in circles.

Touseled

The breeze, soft as autumn
without any hint of winter's bite,
combs hair like a kind toddler–
gentle, without respecting dignity.

Narration

In books we hear thoughts.
A voice tells us what no one knows–
secrets cemented over like an abandoned salt mine,
hopes hidden away from the corrosive air–
we read it all as we follow along their path.
We learn a small shadow of the destination
long before their final punctuation places them to rest.

For good or ill this voice does not haunt our lives.
We step forward into shadow,
without any hint of destination,
hoping that careening feet will meet pavement,
knowing only the steady thump of the present tense.

But sometimes in a quiet moment
after a hug, or a walk past the steadfast tree,
in the silence, though no voice spoke,
we move with reverent step and watchful eye,
for beyond all reason, yet in all certainty,
we hear these words of narration,
"You will not walk this way again."

Apple Dumplings

Five houses from my house
past the small church,
the chain link fence,
and the barking bull dog,
just beyond the telephone poll
covered with an excess of ivy,
which spilled in a green puddle over the sidewalk,
was my park with its swings and slides.
It was the place I pilgrimaged to with my brother
dragging my mother as often as we could.

In truth there was no special grace
imbued into the rust colored plastic
and the stubby little swings.
There was a dingy balance beam
woven between tall evergreen trees,
but the park was otherwise indistinguishable
from any other park except
      I once took my grandmother to that park.

We walked together past the ivy
and the sign for the middle school,
talking about who knows what,
as I showed her my place where I played,
returning the hospitality she had shown at her home.
Her hand around mine, or my brother's,
listening as we showed her our plain park.
We played and walked back.
She made us apple dumplings in our kitchen.
That park was made rich by apple dumplings.

Time

And here we are, a year has passed away,
much has changed, but much remains the same.
The cricket's song has passed to gold,
and there are stories to be told.

Words are capsules waiting in the soil,
a kingdom poised to spring up from its coil.
Two things exist in every day–
the things that will and won't decay.

Pine needles stay for many years;
time will even break down tears.
The soil is richest where homes are built,
where linoleum and carpet both are tilled.

Feet make the best plows.
In time even stone will bow
beneath the presence of a thousand souls.
This is why the bell tolls.

Time sounds in fifteen minute intervals,
An hourly music festival–
sounding the garden's spreading bounds;
silence marks bedlam's hunting grounds.

The battle continues through this age
through the poems born each rising day.
The pine tree grows as the bell divides,
in minutes spread out till the end of time.

Winter's Reprise

Snowfall

Let lilting voices drift like floating snow
on all the flowers gathered here below
in this plot that lies nurtured and unchecked–
a garden grown with equal care, neglect.
Pause for a floating second as the flakes
fly like burning ash with petals in their wake,
drifting down to embers smoking
in the rain, which from the heavens falling,
smites our ears with the pounding, lilting song
that shall fade from earth ere long.
Speak, O voices, before the vision fades,
leaving us like trees–naked and afraid.
We like sheep have gone astray wandering
long from the guiding voice and squandering
the ticking clock on nothing but more clocks,
till with our choir of metronomes we lock
out the soft voices of the choir singing
above.
  Or is it just one, which ringing
down like ashen petals on our soiled gown
settles on our temple like a pearly crown
where like a nesting dove he will ever dwell,
and lilt to our ear that all will be well.

www.ingramcontent.com/pod-product-compliance
Lightning Source LLC
Chambersburg PA
CBHW031503040426
42444CB00007B/1187